MARVEL

ROCKET AND GROOT

TALES OF TERROR

WRITTEN BY
AMANDA DEIBERT

ILLUSTRATED BY
LEO TRINIDAD

SCHOLASTIC

First published by Scholastic in the US, 2024
This edition published by Scholastic in the UK, 2024.
1 London Bridge, London, SE1 9BG
Scholastic Ireland, 89E Lagan Road, Dublin Industrial Estate, Glasnevin, Dublin, D11 HP5

ISBN 978 0702 33960 8

Artwork by Leo Trinidad
Edited by Lori Wieczorek
Lettering by Taylor Esposito
Book design by Martha Maynard

MARVEL

Lauren Bisom, Senior Editor, Juvenile Publishing
Caitlin O'Connell, Associate Editor
Jeremy West, Manager, Licensed Publishing
Sven Larsen, VP Licensed Publishing
C.B. Cebulski, Editor in Chief

A CIP catalogue record for this book is available from the British Library.

Printed in the UK by Bell and Bain Ltd, Glasgow
Paper made from wood grown in sustainable managed forests and other controlled sources.

1 3 5 7 9 10 8 6 4 2

www.scholastic.co.uk

MIX
Paper | Supporting
responsible forestry
FSC
www.fsc.org
FSC® C007785

CHAPTER ONE

6

WHAT ARE YOU DOING?! LET US OUT OF HERE!

IT'S NOT ME. IT'S THE FOREST. IT DEMANDS PAYMENT FOR PASSAGE.

YOU'RE NOT TAKING ALL OUR HARD-EARNED UNITS, BUT-

NOT PAYMENTS IN UNITS. PAYMENTS IN *FEAR.*

I AM GROOT?

NO, NOT SCARE YOU. *YOU* HAVE TO SCARE THE CLEARING. WITH A TERRIFYING STORY.

YOU SPEAK GROOT? WHO ARE YOU?

THE BETTER QUESTION IS "WHO ARE *YOU?*" AND WHAT STORIES DO YOU HAVE TO TELL?

YOU AREN'T READY FOR MY SCARIEST STORIES.

THEN TELL ME ONE YOU THINK WILL BE ENOUGH TO APPEASE THE FOREST.

CHAPTER TWO

23

CHAPTER THREE

33

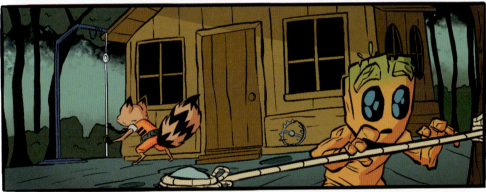

MUNCH
MUNCH
MUNCH

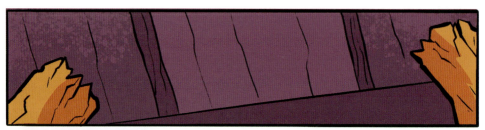

CHAPTER FOUR

OHHHHH ...
YOU ARE FEELING
VERY HUNGRY.

IN A MOST
UNAPPEALING
WAY.

NO EATING. ONLY
SLEEEEPPPP.

YOUR COMBAT
STYLE IS HIGHLY
UNSATISFYING.

WAIT, WHY CAN THE PHOBIATS LEAVE, IF THE REST OF US ARE TRAPPED HERE?

HAVE *YOU* EVER SEEN ANYTHING MORE TERRIFYING?

GOOD POINT.

THAT WAS INVIGORATING. I SINGLE-HANDEDLY DEFEATED OUR FOE IN COMBAT.

SINGLE-HANDEDLY?

I ALLOWED YOU TO HELP. IT IS GOOD FOR YOUR SPIRIT TO FEEL USEFUL.

OKAY, WE'VE RESCUED OUR CUTE LITTLE FRIENDS FROM WHAT I ASSUME HAD TO BE A SELF-INFLICTED PREDICAMENT.

I AM NOT "CUTE." I AM HANDSOME AND FEROCIOUS! BUT GROOT IS ADORABLE.

SURE. LET'S GO.

WE CAN'T.

YOU HAVE A SENTIMENTAL ATTACHMENT TO THIS WEIRD GRAVEYARD?

NO, IT JUST WON'T LET US LEAVE.

HE IS FEELING SCARED. AND SAD.

I AM *NOT!* I JUST NEED A SCARY STORY.

CHAPTER FIVE

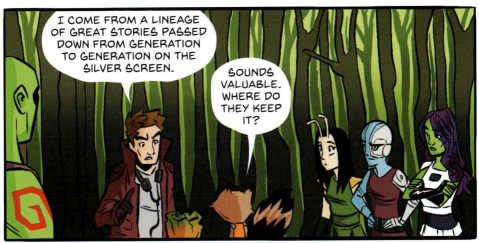

MAYBE IT HAS A SCARY ENDING? DOES PETER DEFEAT THE WITCH, WHO SEEMS SO EASILY HIS SUPERIOR IN EVERY WAY?

HEY!

A COOL FINISHING MOVE?

WELL, HE ... SPILLS A GLASS OF WATER ON HER.

I'M MELLLTTTINNG.

I AM GROOT?!

WHAT?!

DEFEATED BY GOOD HYDRATION. I DON'T BELIEVE IT.

THAT IS NOT A WORTHY END.

THE WITCH WAS THE BEST CHARACTER. SHE SHOULD HAVE WON.

NO ONE IN THE GALAXY APPRECIATES CLASSIC CINEMA.

DON'T WORRY, STAR-LORD. A BEING MUST EXIST WHO WOULD LIKE YOUR TERRIBLE STORY. PERHAPS SOMEWHERE OVER THE RAINBOW.

IT IS HIDEOUS. BUT I THINK IT MEANS WE CAN LEAVE.

WHAT DO YOU MEAN?

YOUR BIGGEST FEAR IS CAPTIVITY. FOR YOU AND THOSE YOU LOVE MOST. NOW I AM WEARING IT. WE WILL BE ABLE TO GO.

YEAH, HONESTLY, HE FIGURED IT OUT. YOU CAN LEAVE.

SEE? MAYBE I HAVE THE COURAGE *AND* THE BRAINS.

IF ONLY I COULD FIGURE OUT IF YOU WERE MADE OF COUCHES OR POTATO?

CREATOR BIOS

AMANDA DEIBERT IS A *NEW YORK TIMES* BESTSELLING COMIC BOOK AND TELEVISION WRITER. HER COMIC BOOK WRITING INCLUDES STAR WARS HYPERSPACE STORIES (LUCASFILM); DARKWING DUCK (DISNEY/DYNAMITE); DC SUPER HERO GIRLS, TEEN TITANS GO!, WONDER WOMAN '77, BATMAN AND SCOOBY-DOO!, *LOVE IS LOVE* (NYT #1 BESTSELLER) AND MORE FOR DC COMICS; JOHN CARPENTER'S TALES FOR A HALLOWEENIGHT, VOLUMES 2–8 (STORM KING COMICS); AND MORE. HER TELEVISION WORK INCLUDES *HE-MAN AND THE MASTERS OF THE UNIVERSE* FOR NETFLIX AND FOUR YEARS AS A WRITER FOR FORMER VICE PRESIDENT AL GORE'S INTERNATIONAL CLIMATE BROADCAST, *24 HOURS OF REALITY.*

LEO TRINIDAD IS A *NEW YORK TIMES* BESTSELLING ILLUSTRATOR AND ANIMATOR FROM COSTA RICA. FOR 15 YEARS HE HAS BEEN CREATING CONTENT FOR CHILDREN'S BOOKS AND TV SHOWS. HE HAS WORKED AS A STORYBOARD ARTIST FOR ANIMATED SHOWS PRODUCED BY DISNEY, DREAMWORKS AND CARTOON NETWORK. LEO IS KNOWN FOR BEING THE CREATOR OF THE FIRST ANIMATED SERIES EVER PRODUCED IN CENTRAL AMERICA. IN 2018, HE WON FIRST PLACE IN THE CENTRAL AMERICAN GRAPHIC NOVEL CONTEST, ORGANIZED BY THE FRENCH ALLIANCE OF COSTA RICA.

LOVED ROCKET AND GROOT: TALES
OF TERROR? KEEP READING FOR A TEASER OF
SPIDER-HAM: HOLLYWOOD MAY-HAM!

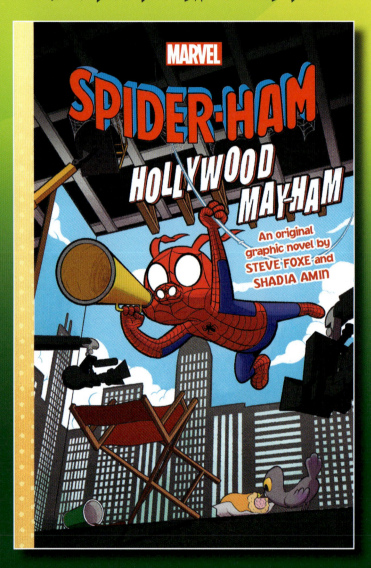

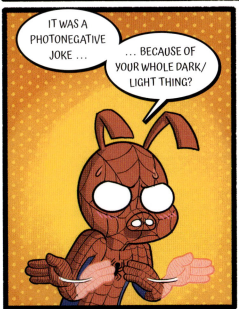

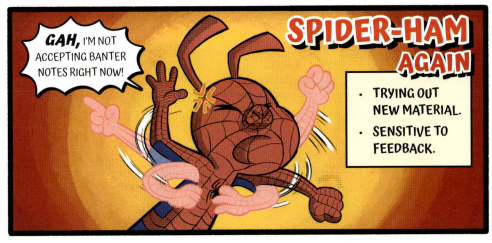